Two Dying Lovers Holding a Cat *sounds like a work of portraiture: a subject closely observed, elaborated into vivid, arresting life.*

That subject is a very particular queer love, one that Costa renders both with tenderness and shamelessness – at turns eros, at turns agape, decadent in all the senses of that word. That also makes it a stark piece of melancholia, but the kind of melancholia you'd want to take a bath in.

No mean feat – these poems make of the reader a lateral thinker, finding lush beauty in sadness, richness in absence, colour and taste and music in places colour and taste and music ought not to be, and in language they ought not to be in. This book made me blush, and it surprised me, and it hurt in the very finest way.

David Nash, author of *The Islands of Chile*

Two Dying Lovers Holding a Cat *is a stunning debut that charts love and loss, honouring scenes between lovers that are at once unique and recognisable, and heightened in memory.*

Costa's deeply intimate work invites us not only to read, but to share in feeling. These poems are propelled by their quiet music; Costa's talent for precise language and rich imagery is palpable.

These are poems of abundance – of the natural world, of emotion and of the body – heady with the taste, scent and colour of wine, vermouth, orange zest, and morello cherry.

Lauren Garland, author of *Darling*

Luís Costa's debut pamphlet woke me up last night. I couldn't stop thinking about the lines: "what if I am lighting / candles for the living". Costa has a way of writing about difficult feelings in a beautiful way; I feel less alone in my queerness knowing that Costa is writing poems about queer love for us all.

Jo Morris Dixon, author of *I Told You Everything*

First published in 2023 by Fourteen Publishing.
fourteenpoems.com

Design and typeset by Stromberg Design.
strombergdesign.co.uk

Proofreading and copy editing by Lara Kavanagh.
lk-copy.com

Printed by Print2Demand Ltd, Westoning, Bedfordshire, UK.

Luís Costa has asserted their right to be identified as the author of this work in accordance with the Copyright, Designs and Patents Act 1988.

This book is sold subject to the conditions that it shall not be lent, resold, hired out or otherwise circulated without the publisher's prior consent. Any republishing of the individual works must be agreed in advance.

ISBN:
978-1-7391697-7-0

two dying lovers holding a cat

Luís Costa

contents:

Chronogram
-

Antegrade
Retrograde

Of course he smells like lemons
Harvest

Homeland
Invasion

Summer Storm
Equinox

Nocturne in D Minor
Curtain Call

Matutine
Vespertine

Good Friday

Rotation
Thirty-Eight Past Nine

Lipiec/July
Listopad/November

Souvenir
Stoned at the big Sainsbury's

Ascension
Ornithomancy

Recitativo
Aria

Emulsion
Feast of All Saints

-

Two Dying Lovers   *Holding a Cat*

CHRONOGRAM

All this time,
          we were the moths.
In pants and socks.
               Shirts on the
bedroom floor.
           One day they will
make a film about us.
               Chasing
candles, baking tarts.
               We have
danced around the dust.
               And so
I have loved you,
           dawn through
dusk,
      quivering wings rising in
teeth,
    sugar,
        peach, and
            tongue.

ANTEGRADE

Sundown leaks into the apartment,
a passion

fruit hue shrouds him slowly.
(He dreams of violins and gardenias.

When I'm sad
I dream of plane crashes.) Maybe

I travel to the day Dolores left
so I don't have to feel the rain
on the night he will.

Should I take a photograph or choose
to remember? Maybe
next November, when I open
my birthday wine (six days too early).

There will be fireworks in his eyes,
and a purple glare from the off license sign
painting his face,

now the map of a country
that no longer exists. He would whisper

we must break the leaves, light

the bonfires. Maybe

next November he will be striding:
it only drizzles but
he is buying his new boyfriend
non-celebratory wine (his mother died).

Hands under the jumper, I hold him now,
bearing music
in new gardens. It would be easier
if we could let this twilight burn but

there is a cat we will not adopt
(and that we never called Manhattan).

Surely
we are still young,
and it's the night that's getting old.

RETROGRADE

June brought thyme into my garden.
I hear Christmas carols,
your golden hair
speckled by the hail, eyelashes a frosted
fence for the blue.
My clothes are smoke, the air is melting.
Hawkish wind bites
the knuckles, draws blood from the neck.
In from frigid lands, far from the bloom,
the blaze, the blades of grass,
your absence
seeped into my sheets again.
Arms content, sinking the bed
into ice, soaking cotton, bursting
dreams of rivers cold as your collarbones.
You are coming for my lungs.
These glacial hymns, whispering flakes,
expired devotion,
they speak in a language
I no longer understand.
The almond blossoms
turn to snow, white oceans swell
as mist from the forests where
our bodies lie together now.

OF COURSE HE SMELLS LIKE LEMONS

His face licked by the pink of neon lights,
green marble eyes
watching our warming beers in the dark.
Under this table,
shielded from the bright stars, his leg hair
dances to Chopin
waltzes in my palm. And I want to drink
him so slowly, hard
jawlines that softly simmer in this tender
night. Four hundred
days since I imagined air around his bed,
to melt in the sheets
of merengue wrapping his thighs. Our day
will come, he tells me;
I did not kiss him for the last time just yet.

HARVEST

you,
        a vertiginous razor.
me,
pomegranate seeds
        coating autumnal days.
I stare into the wide abyss
of your face,
drinking
the cascading
    beauty
        of what
            we could have been
    today. I watch you count
three silent minutes
    of meticulous tooth-brushing.

you,
the beginning of spring,
    scaffolding water lilies,
flirting shades of pink
    over sharp edges of the Vistula.

me,
carrying
  this fear that I, a prolific
      swimmer, will very likely drown.

HOMELAND

I return
        to the vineyards
        of your body
craving plums,
        honeysuckle and red.

I've been fasting
        for too long,
    my love,
and my lips grow
        weary with emptiness.

Perhaps I know
        which roots
contain you,
or perhaps I wander like   crickets in the night.

You always grow
        the largest branches in
the scorched
    earth

            within my heart –

INVASION

Eleven o'clock strikes with

its chaotic optimism   and air raid sirens.

Decanting wine in

my green tracksuit,   I am deep ruby too.

Notes of gift-wrapped delusion.

The parabolic acidity

          leeches on my bruises.

          But the grip is

waning, as springtime   emerges yawning

daffodils all over the parks.

One hour from

now we will breathe   into the mountains.

SUMMER STORM   *to Witold*

Tiptoeing, we are mushrooms bleeding
at the edges of the cliff,
a supplicant stride into the castles, steps
crunching the branches
orphaned by gales. In your arms I will
be moss again, gently
growing by the streams born in the back
of our necks. I want to
kiss you in all the places we've never seen:
dark ravines, clear ponds,
dense orchards of plum trees. We will beg
to burn under violet
skies, craving thunder, the arrival of your
rain. And we must dream,
gliding like eagles that coast on borrowed bikes.
Tonight, your colours
found their way into my heart: this red
of Polish berries, tongue
dancing with cream, your teeth yearning
to drip down my bare
chest. After I'm gone, leave your window
open, summer storms
will bring me back to you.

EQUINOX

Twelve times these stitches burst, one by one.
The wound bleeds over
the mantelpiece, looped
      tears stain the floors.

  It is Saturday morning,
late September. The last of the summer sun
invades his kitchen, licking
the salt from my stomach. I have figured out
his coffee machine,
      at last.
      Across the counter,
in between the red   carnations that I bought,
      he lies
victorious, my scintillating warrior
from lands whose language I don't
speak. Bare quads peeking through, dark hips
swim in the milk of bedlinen,   lone
volatile
      metronomes.
        I left
around noon, honey-covered lips, pockets
full of sandalwood and musk.

      I can hear him in the night
buses, leaking taps, stumbling drunks. Noises
that scratch my suspended itch.

                    Among

steps, drops, engines, there's silence reminding me

that I was never thunder to his rain. Maybe he was

an orange

and my hands carried his scent   all day long.

NOCTURNE IN D MINOR

You call me in the middle of the night.
Somewhere in Wardour Street my next
lover is kissing another man. I pretend
to be asleep, you whisper words of lead.
The ceiling drips, brow tingles, suddenly
the moon tastes of blood & it smells like
your grey wedding suit. Someone should
photograph me dying here, underneath
the canopies, wearing only my favourite
cashmere jumper. This light is the mother
of all quietude, at this hour the glass cracks
triumphantly, there's honey in your voice.
Onyx skies infiltrate these forests & I am
reminded of shiny droplet constellations
sparkling on your chest hair as chainmail
after you shower. The phone still chimes
as the blossoming bells of my hometown.
It is late, a desolated Manhattan bar sees
another ex swallow vodka martinis (three
olives) cold as perpetual snows, all of this
just before noon; & he googles "psychics
near me" – they will tell him all the things
I once gift-wrapped in little purple parcels:

the fool, knight of swords, reversed tower.
But now I need to paint these walls, a cave
for sirens, glistening with yellow stars from
the ringtone. Rain floods the room until I
answer, turning this bed into a big Scottish
lake. You stare. Etched in the back of your
throat are the things you never said, lonely
aeroplane tickets, intermittent songs of lust
& grief. What do you want, I ask you now.
You say: my love, tonight I could not sleep.

CURTAIN CALL

    Drawing squares in the grass,   we walk across the common,
        sharks in the current. Circles   and triangles have let us down.
    Green always festers, you'd   say. Then there is dampness,
        sometimes ice. Here we will   become a lonely collection
of polaroids. Dusty and bare,   I will keep them away, I fear
        they too will halve. As will a   regular order at the Fentiman
Arms. This last evening, we   drink next to the fire, silently.
        The waitress asks once again   what are we having; I want to tell
her your eyes, your lips,   your ribcage. I want to beg for time to learn the
naked shape   of your body in the dark,
for my breathing, orchestra   tuning, to give you a symphony.
        Order red wine, my Patroclus   in the rain. I shall inhabit this cave,
eating popcorn, with the scent of your fabric conditioner inside
my chest. I do not know how   days turn drizzle into white
        peaches and haze. The nights   we must spend decorating our
pantheon have arrived, we've   birthed an indomitable silence.
See, the things we never said   are now asking for a voice.

MATUTINE

the martyrdom of sunlight
at seven in the morning
tears the Thames
with lavender
blades.

all of this feeding our eyes,

the weight of   the sky threads

my flesh into your bones.

serene
glide, a slow
sentinel, hungrily
wishing to meet this sea
just as I want to possess you.

VESPERTINE

I joined the party,

spilled vermouth

all over you

and your couch. A winter

sky sequestered

by the night   made my coat wet

with sleet

and unforgiveness. You

always know how to make me

leave, ice

ambushed   by the glass.

I never know how to disappear,

kiss

goodbye

men that hold your waist

and pretend   this stain is easy

to remove. It's your red

velour. In a few days

you will barely

see it.

GOOD FRIDAY

Every time   I hold his hand
I'm telling the world:
                      we too
deserve a piece   of sorbet skies,
where old tapestries   sprawl time,
we belong within   the history
of these walls,   we are melodies,
lilac symphonies,   slices of blood
orange in drinks   that soothe our
souls.
    We are worthy.
        We are whole.

ROTATION

There is a lead-in sound then music
invades this space. There used to be
a record shop at the end of our road,

back when we wanted to move away,
live in France or maybe just Fitzrovia,
before you forgot to water our plants.

Underneath the static there is a thread,
a sequence snaking through equations,
counting sweat drops in old armours:

look at us, sleeping within inconstant
indecisions, amongst unpacked bags,
melting window frost, broken clocks.

I now hear the wine bleeding darkly
into glass, like the drumroll from lips,
emboldened pink, leaning for a kiss.

Lightly, in my mouth, our words dance
and tomorrow rumbles, afraid to arrive.
This is the first Sunday we'll ever have.

THIRTY-EIGHT PAST NINE

It rains. Your husband-to-be is picking
you up from Victoria station.
I must see your shadows
leave,
warm shepherds falling asleep. Yesterday,
you chose
a wedding suit and a tie
to match the green fires in his eyes
when he watches you
come
quietly, his forest of light growing inside
your body.
And today, you and I
mourn
untaken roads, half-eaten
chocolate bars in the back seat of the car,
a Kate Bush song you once
loved
too. My wet jacket is folded at my feet,
tomorrow I give
you up again,
if tomorrow comes – time was always
yours to
take.

LIPIEC/JULY

I long to be a cherry in the lips
of my lover. Sinking deep in his
blood, flowing
into the ocean under the skin
to crash my waves, exhaling
onto the rocks
where intrepid flowers grow.
I also beg for the end
of his sword, to become desert
wind blazing
skies as summer
turns forests into fire, embers,
ash. I too long to be bitten
as almonds from my homeland,
or to drip down his chin
like dark figs.
Above all,
I want to be made
of Californian grapes
ripening in the ginger
warmth of his never-ending sun.

LISTOPAD/NOVEMBER

I am now a photograph, yellow
as your corduroy disappearing
down the road,
into the gust.

For too long, we feasted on birds,
swarmed by tides
of weary lies
that decorate the airport stairs.

Your sleepy eyes were an estuary
where my light was reflected
to the city,

I translated its colours,
composed our lullabies. Between
the mountains we became,
sand
turned
to glass
at last.

How tall do cypresses grow
here
in the graveyard
of our love?

SOUVENIR

His back against the marble,
    sturdy spine of tall
encyclopaedias holding the colossal saffron walls.

Under this brazen Tuscan sun,
slow sweat drips
down wheat fields of golden hair between clouds
of his linen shirt, buttons undone.
                          One, two, three.

It's my face versus the gelato.
Olive skin and morello
cherry, dark chocolate.   *Aren't those your favourites?*

I will tell him a secret:
                *only the wind moves the way
you do.* His eyes like samphire watch the gelato win.

My back against his palms,   he licks my beard clean.

STONED AT THE BIG SAINSBURY'S

I notice how forgetfulness grows
        in the frost around ice-cream tubs
        and melts into saccharine oblivion.
        Why do the peaches smell bold
        this year. Or is it that my teeth are dry
and lonely. The salt corridors are here,
        these altars which I've never seen, remind me
        of your body building roads to facilitate
        the occupation. As aspirant mangoes,
I am here waiting to be lifted, licked
        and loved. But all the hands drop fuel
        like planes before a crash. I walk ahead,
        my chest creaks as ships sailing through,
wild arpeggios of tarragon. And there you
should be, holding me, playing me, your
        cello. In the end,
        I bought food
        for a cat
        I do not even have.

ASCENSION

heading south is the man
whose sweat I've wished for.
he who left   indelible stains
in my five-hundred-thread-
-count sheets.
rampant cosmic deity, I am
wind inside his veins.
fire holds these wrists, I stab
his chest with kisses.
            teeth like
stars, anchored legs, unyielding
embrace.
supple tongues travelling down
crests to reach the sea,
    lips wet
with leftover
wine from the banquets,
piercing   the Trojan walls,
longing, warm,
waiting. we are ash.
now living incessantly
in a lurid   space
between   the gentle seasons.

ORNITHOMANCY

We are watching planes in the park,
following currents, lost and found;
Helens of Troy rescued before ants
climb over our backs. Heat gathers,
men wipe forehead sweat with their
boyfriends' t-shirts. Not you – I am
a haunting, imagining the quiet trails
towards your chest. I have borrowed
this: cloud jigsaws and the glistening
dust, machines ascend and descend
to deliver promised embraces as birds
honour floating flares and burnt bites.
Our lungs emerge, these emerald blades
tame the hammerheads circling down,
trickling as thick sap inside the birch,
water which flows into the glass, a tongue
in the lips, dreams that hold entire skies.
Away from the daisies my legs crushed,
you will pretend we can contain the blue
as our summer mouths swallow the flights.

RECITATIVO

it is written in his tongue:
        the abundance of pleasure,
all of Bach's cantatas,
        the sunsets over Florence
which glaze statues
        in luminous shades
        of caramel.

it is etched in his eyes:
        radiant forests,
glorious mazes, jasmine
and gold,
        moonlit staircases
        in old white palaces,
        velvet cloaks against
naked skin.

it is mapped in his neck:
        the echoes of Greek lyres
and Lisbon's jacarandas,
deep amber   and orange zest.

it is burning in the core
        of the most devoted skies.

ARIA

waiting for the 87 to Wandsworth Town,
getting further away from a stranger's flat,
his saliva still drying on my neck, smoking
a stale cigarette (stolen from a drag queen),
and his very stubborn aftershave is clinging
to my hands as I try to wipe trainers dirty
from the dancefloors, while carrying vestiges
of a sore head from that cheap
wine I drank in your arms in Vauxhall Park
before I decided that you knew the names
of all the trees, even the ones which you
may have never seen before this afternoon –
you left impeccably slow like New Year's
day, a myriad of blue evaporating deep into
the city, vanishing inside the same shades
of concrete that now see me go home alone.

EMULSION

it starts with him
covered in   flour
then licking
a spoon   in the kitchen

I was melting
butter and the counter
is demanding
weight   or a spill

    I scratch
the neck the shoulder the back
with my stubble

the bulbs are waiting
for the knife   he grabs my
hips   the garlic sizzles

he stirs   me inside
swiftly dripping   I am his

a feline light
an open flame
bursting   across his face

FEAST OF ALL SAINTS

Autumn always deals
in sharp fragrances.
What if I told you
that your noise still
lives inside my head.
What if I am lighting
candles for the living.
November never comes
fast and often lingers.
I contemplate the density
of the earth. We are
half ready,
half bruised. I am
wholly seduced
by the loud emptiness
at your seat.

TWO DYING LOVERS   HOLDING A CAT

Remember the time, thirty-nine past

    eight, swallow its eloping darkness
as we surrender to the dusk. Curious

    hearts tend to be drenched in stars.
You are picking the cherries. Look

    outside, lamps are blossoming, see
how they form shy constellations?

    Do we dare to fly one last time? I
charted a city we never called our

    home. It was a frail shield, a flicker
of dawn. The siege is over, we have

    bled enough to die. Your mother's
watch conducts our melody (tick),

    glistening (tock) on the bedside table,
infinite bars living inside each hour.

    I bought whiskey. Remember when
spring filled this space with flowers?

    Now everything is red, everywhere is
plumbeous. We have finished the night

    caps, let's turn off the light. There is
another house in which we are the cat.

    No one is drinking poison. Tonight
faints like condensation in this glass.

    We know it. Tomorrow never comes.

Notes and Acknowledgements

Many thanks to Ben Townley-Canning at *fourteen poems* for publishing my debut pamphlet and for being the best first editor I could have hoped for.

My gratitude to the editors of the following journals and literary magazines, in which some of these poems first appeared, sometimes in different formats: *INKSOUNDS, Stone of Madness, Visual Verse*, and *Queerlings*. Thank you to the judges of the 2022 Out-Spoken Prize for Poetry for longlisting the poem "Invasion".

Thank you also to Jack Westmore for his always generous feedback and for believing in my poems from the beginning. For their beautiful friendship and support, a warm thank you to Samuel White, Abi Kendall, Sarah White, and Michał Ozdarski. A very special thank you to Henry Clifford, for his ingenuity and encouragement.

Lastly, my most heartfelt gratitude to Witold Wójciak, *ta książka jest dla Ciebie*.

"Chronogram" was first published in *INKSOUNDS* Journal 4.
"Of course he smells like lemons" was first published in Issue 19 of *Stone of Madness*.
"Nocturne in D Minor" was first published in *Visual Verse*, vol. 9, ch. 9.
"Good Friday" was first published in *Queerlings* (Issue 6).